Praying with the Benedic

Dave,
May this little book of prayer remind you of the times you have spent at Saint Meinrad and in southern Indiana. May it offer hope, consolation and guidance on your spiritual journey. Happy 55th! _Da[illegible]

For Archabbot Justin Duvall and the monks of
St. Meinrad Archabbey.

Praying with the Benedictines

A Window on the Cloister

Guerric DeBona, OSB

FOREWORD BY

Joan Chittister, OSB

Paulist Press
New York/Mahwah, NJ

Cover photo: Brother Jonah Ponder, OSB, of St. Meinrad Archabbey, St. Meinrad, Indiana

Stained glass windows on page i and on page 56 designed by Dom Gregory deWit, OSB, of Mont Cesar Abbey, Louvain, Belgium; manufactured by Emil Frei of St. Louis, Missouri

Paintings of monks on page facing Foreword and on pp. 4, 18, and 33: Brother Martin Erspamer, OSB, of St. Meinrad Archabbey, St. Meinrad, Indiana

For a list of acknowledgments and permissions, see p. 63.

Cover and book design by Lynn Else

Library of Congress Cataloging-in-Publication Data

DeBona, Guerric, 1955–
Praying with the Benedictines : a window on the cloister / Guerric DeBona ; foreword by Joan Chittister.
p. cm.
Includes index.
ISBN 978-0-8091-4443-3 (alk. paper)
1. Benedictines—Prayer-books and devotions—English. 2. Catholic Church—Prayer-books and devotions—English. I. Title.
BX2050.B46D43 2007
271′.1—dc22

2006034155

Published by Paulist Press
997 Macarthur Boulevard
Mahwah, New Jersey 07430

www.paulistpress.com

Printed and bound in the
United States of America

Contents

Foreword

Some people ask, "How are we supposed to pray?" Other people ask—more correctly, I think—"How do *you* pray?" Prayer, you see, is a very personal part of spiritual development. It changes as we change. It deepens as we grow. It simplifies as we do, as the years go by.

Prayer centers us and stretches us and lays us bare, as the prayer says, "of all our self-conceits." Inside ourselves, we know who we are and what we need and what we lack and what we don't understand and what we long for as we go. It is this awareness and the dependence on God it brings with it that are the wellspring of prayer.

Those thoughts, if we honor them and face them, become the foundation of a prayer life that will eventually strip us of everything but our desire for God. Prayer is the awareness that it is not a question of whether or not God is present to us—that we can take for granted; instead, prayer is the process of *our* becoming present to God.

So, real prayer can be fed by any one of a number of things—scripture, nature, personal experience, emotional pressures, intellectual commitment to the God who is greater than any idea of God we can possibly have. But whatever the life-link that brings us into consciousness of God, in the end the way we each pray has something to do with who we are.

The whole notion, then, that there is some prayer formula or ritual or schedule or style that is right for everyone is, at best, naive. Even the *Rule* of Benedict, that sixth-century document on the spiritual life that devotes more chapters to prayer than to any other topic in the Rule, ends the long outline of psalms and readings by saying, "But if any of the monastics know a better way, let them arrange them differently." No single form, we find, is the ultimate valuation of a life of prayer. And in another place Benedict says, "Let prayer be short and pure unless, perhaps, it is lengthened by divine grace." The purpose of choral prayer, it is clear, is simply to inspire personal prayer.

It cannot be surprising, then, that Benedictines—however much they have all been formed in a lifetime of daily choral recitation of psalms and scriptures, day after day, year after year of their entire monastic life—will at the same time find that ongoing river of biblical insights simply the beginning of their own personal spiritual journey to the God within.

Guerric DeBona's *Praying with the Benedictines* is actually a glimpse into the endgame of the spiritual life for lifelong monastics, all of whom have taken the trek into the Spirit together, and yet each of whom has experienced it differently and alone—must we all.

This little book is a treasure-house of personal glimpses into God. May it feed and deepen your own. Like everything else in life, that is its only purpose. And, in the end, that is the truest form of prayer there can possibly be.

Joan Chittister, OSB
May 2006

Introduction

Benedictine prayer has been something like a great, symphonic river for the church for over fifteen hundred years. Like a hidden spring, Christian monasticism found its source in the desert plains of Egypt some years before Benedict of Nursia (AD 480–547) founded his monastery first in Subiaco and then in Monte Casino. The man who would become the patron of Western Europe reinvigorated an entire civilization by bringing both discipline and moderation to those men and women seeking God in solitude, silence, and community life. Benedict's *Rule* for monks is a remarkable document notable for its psychological perception and practical wisdom. The *Rule* has quietly traversed the lives of countless generations, even as Benedictine monasticism has been expressed in a variety of interpretations over the ages; its instruction has given life to a world that has produced saints, scholars, teachers, mystics, prophets, musicians, poets, preachers, bishops, popes, and thousands of other vocations that have labored in the Lord's vineyard. Above all else, the sons and daughters of St. Benedict have been the church at prayer: creation freely returning to the Creator the life-giving love bestowed on us in Christ. Benedictine public and private prayer is an ebb and flow of petition, thanksgiving, praise, and adoration into the ocean of God's merciful love. As the wonderful poet and mystic Hildegard of Bingen said so well in her Antiphon for St. Boniface, "The living light / watched you water your gardens / as a wise man hastens / the course of pure streams / that flow from God back to God."

Benedictine prayer is the church with its hands outstretched to God; this reality has been astonishingly diverse and creative, drawing from a rich scriptural and ecclesial tradition within the contexts of historical circumstances. The Liturgy of the Hours as it has been chanted by monks and nuns in the West for centuries is perhaps most familiar to the world at large, yet the Benedictine experience courses through a much wider landscape than even the gorgeous modal settings of plain song. The encounter with God in the desert reveals a prayer watering the full bloom of both liturgical and private prayer. Benedictine prayer has labored with the yoke of obedience and scaled the ladder of humility, all the while encouraging an expanding heart that loves before all else and, finally, casts out fear. As they pursue the search for God, monks and nuns thrive on the world of everyday living. The landscape of the ordinary transforms simple men and women into companions of God, mystics consoled by the unfathomable encounter with Christ, ever new and ever radiant in the paschal mystery.

The present collection is a very modest attempt to render Benedictines at prayer. It would be impossible to represent accurately the full range of monastic prayer in such a collection. But if I have suggested that monastic prayer has been a river to God's people, the collection that follows is something of a quiet, meandering stream. The opening selection, taken from the Prologue of the *Rule of St. Benedict,* invites monks and all Christians to follow the Lord in a way that runs with single-hearted devotion. The various selections from the *Holy Rule* that follow remain something of a constant in this book, lovely bright stones that reflect the light in the passing of time, that hint at the shimmering radiance of the journey to God. Taken together, the passages begin with some meditations on the monastic virtues of obedience and humility, wind into exhortations on work and tools for good works, ripple over exhortations on liturgical and contemplative prayer, and then flow into the reflections on the prayerful peace that comes from a graced union with God. At the same time, each of the selections mirrors a particular cultural frame and religious piety and may also be read profitably as individual selections for *lectio divina*. Ultimately, *Praying with the Benedictines* is meant to be a companion on life's journey for all those seeking the Lord—wherever we may be—so that we might be mindful of the God who blesses all creation. In the words of Psalm 1, then, the entire Christian community might be "like a tree that is planted beside the flowing waters that yields its fruit in due season." With that in mind, we Benedictines continue to pray "that in all things God may be glorified."

BEDE
ULRICH

Praying with the Benedictines

The Call

It is to find workers in his cause that God calls out like that to all peoples. He calls to us in another way in the psalm when he says, Who is there with a love of true life and a longing for days of real fulfillment [Ps 34:12]? If you should hear that call and answer, "I," this is the answer you will receive from God: If you wish to have that true life that lasts for ever, then keep your tongue from evil; let your lips speak no deceit; turn away from wrongdoing; seek out peace and pursue it [Ps 34:13–14]. If you do that, he says, I shall look on you with such love and my ears will be so alert to your prayer that, before you so much as call on me, I shall say to you: Here I am [Is 58:9]. What gentler encouragement could we have, my dear brothers and sisters, than that word from the Lord calling us to himself in such a way! We can see with what loving concern the Lord points out to us the path of life [Ps 16:11].

And so to prepare ourselves for the journey before us, let us renew our faith and set ourselves high standards by which to lead our lives. The gospel should be our guide in following the way of Christ to prepare ourselves for his presence in the kingdom to which he has called us [1 Thess 2:12].

—*Rule of St. Benedict,* Prologue

The Burning Bush

There is fire in the Rule of Saint Benedict. Every page of the book you are holding in your hands proves this conclusion. To reappropriate the meaning of the "Holy Rule" as Benedictine monastics have called it throughout the centuries, one needs to take off one's shoes and stand on the holy ground on which Benedict stood when he wrote this text. We wear, each one of us, our own shoes or sandals. They differ from person to person, from tradition to tradition. We have developed a surprising variety of footwear, but the holy ground on which we tread is the same.

—David Steindl-Rast, OSB

The Rule and Meditation

In Benedictine monasteries the Rule is read daily, but only a very short passage each day. The Rule is like an old, fully-bodied red wine; it is best enjoyed in sips. A person who exceeds moderation, or does not know how to drink with discernment, is to be pitied. Head and heart, soul and spirit ought to relish the words of the Rule, just as the eye is gladdened at the colour of the wine, while the tongue, sense of smell and palate—each in its own way—savour the precious gift of God. If one has tasted on the tongue a maxim of Benedict's by repeating it over and over to oneself, one will reflect further, follow it up by meditating on biblical words, parables or characters which suggest themselves to us. Or by meditating on the Person, the mystery, and the teaching of Jesus.

—Abbot George Holzherr

Mutual Obedience

Obedience is of such value that it should be shown not only to the superior, but also to all members of the community; in fact, they should be obedient to each other, in the sure knowledge that this way of obedience is the one that will take them straight to God.

—*Rule of St. Benedict* 71

Self-Will

Obedience is a defense against self-will: no wolf is cleverer at assuming sheep's clothing than the wolf of self-will. What St. Benedict says about this defect sends a chill down the spine. It seems to go against what we call today self-expression, self-fulfillment, and the rest. But he has a point here. It is easy to make ourselves the center of our own little universe, to live our lives for our own self-aggrandizement, our own self-gratification. "Good" people fall into this trap. In their zeal they try to compete with others, trample them underfoot. Do not be so sure that the teaching of St. Benedict on self-will is out of date. Experience shows us how subtly, very subtly, we can seek... "self." The art of being a Christian and therefore the art of being a monk, is to learn to put God at the center—the love of God and of our neighbor; to be devoted to God and to our neighbor. You meet people who apparently are very spiritual, very holy—only to detect, on closer acquaintance, that self-seeking takes precedence over seeking God or the service of their neighbor.

—Cardinal Basil Hume, OSB

lical Openness

)bedient creativity is very demanding. Because I am in the dance, because the dance is the life of the Trinity flowing through creation, I receive only to give, and in giving I receive again and the more there is to give. If I have listened to the word I may also be asked to speak it, and I cannot be selective in the speaking any more than in the listening, though there is the endless search to know and understand what speaking is demanded by the delicacy of love. And here again there is a poverty at the heart of things, because the creative act that has been beautiful and blessed cannot be repeated. It was a unique beauty and I cannot cling to it lest I degrade it; I must give it away and go on living, and try to be open to the new thing that the Lord God will do.

—Maria Boulding, OSB

Real Perfection

In itself the Rule and all its material prescriptions are something altogether exterior and therefore accessory and secondary in the work of our sanctification. One could be perfect in exterior observance and yet be an unworthy monk. But obedience, though it is a small thing in relation to God, like all human things, acquires an almost infinite value if it is practiced with love.

—Abbot Columba Marmion, OSB

The Qualities of the Abbot

The abbot or abbess should reflect on the significance of their own high status in the monastery and remember the meaning of the title they bear. They should be aware of what is meant by the saying that more is demanded of those to whom more is entrusted. They should reflect on what a difficult and demanding task they have accepted, namely, that of guiding souls and serving the needs of so many different characters; gentle encouragement will be needed for one, strong rebukes for another, rational persuasion for another, according to the character and intelligence of each. It is the task of the superiors to adapt with sympathetic understanding to the needs of each so that they may not only avoid any loss but even have the joy of increasing the number of good sheep in the flock committed to them.

—*Rule of St. Benedict* 2

Monastic Mission

The monastic community shares in the mission of the Church first of all by the life it lives. Monks reveal God to one another and to the world, taking up the strong, bright weapons of obedience to seek him in faith through prayer, work, silence, asceticism, a common life in peace. They carry forward the gospel tradition by love and mutual service, especially attentive, through their Divine Office and holy reading, to the voice of the Spirit in Sacred Scripture. By refusing to trust itself to the world or to be seduced by the values of an earthly kingdom, the monastic community proclaims that the world as we know it is passing away, and bears witness to a kingdom visible only to the eyes of faith.

—Members of the Swiss-American Congregation

The Expanding Heart

We need to reassess our lives in the light of the two great Commandments of Jesus, using the resources of our Benedictine spirituality. We who have prayed much may be called to shift the balance to service, we who have been hospitable may be called to withdraw in silent prayer, we who have been still may be called to study. The purpose of this testing is to make us sensitive to the spirit at work in our hearts and so be schooled to love God and others more creatively.

—Kym Harris, OSB

SUSCIPE ME, DOMINE,
SECUNDUM ELOQUIUM TUUM,
ET VIVAM.
ET NON CONFUNDAS ME
AB EXPECTATIONE MEA.

—From the *Rite of Profession* and Psalm 118:116

(Uphold me, O Lord, according to your promise and I shall live. And do not confound me in my expectation.)

Stability of Heart

The spiritual value of stability lies in commitment. Like everything else in monastic life, stability works best when it is wholehearted, without escape hatches or preserves of autonomy. Having committed both spiritual and material fate to a particular community, a Benedictine has a stake in keeping the community focused on what they are meant to be about. She must be faithful to the Work of God, *lectio divina,* personal prayer. She has committed herself to being present to her sisters in the monastery. She works in support of their life together. She attends chapters and community meetings, welcomes guests and newcomers to the community. She helps to care for those who are ill or in distress, and helps to bury the dead. She works at seeing Christ in the people with whom she lives. Where better to find him?

—Columba Stewart, OSB

My Choice

I chose a rather smallish world,
high on a smallish hill,
where I could mill it day by day
to taste its mint and dill.

The biggish world has laughed a lot,
it thinks I chose too small,
but I have secret microscopes
that make my world grow tall—

Right past the birds and through the clouds
and higher than the sky
and deeper too till that be up;
I hardly have to try.

The smallest bit that comes my way
I take into my eye
and find in it a simple food
to feed this hungry spy.

The fun of it has made me laugh—
the monster bugs and flowers
that grow up big and fat and tall
and gobble up the hours.

By seeing smaller I have grown
to be my very size—
the image of an unseen God
who makes me too to rise.

—Harry Hagan, OSB

Monastic Witness

We can say that the monastery as a place of community and grace is an assembly in Christ, a gathering in the name of Christ. St. Benedict calls the monastery the "House of God" (RB 31.19; 53.22: 64.5). It is the place where his Word is enthroned and proclaimed, where monks seek the presence and glory of God, where Christ is represented in the abbot, the sick and the guests. It is the place where believers are already in communion with Christ and expect to be brought forward into the communion of eternal life: "Let them... prefer nothing whatever to Christ, and may he bring us all together to everlasting life" (RB 72.1–12). Communion in Christ is a grace, and the goal of the communion is continual life with God in Christ. The monastery, as a group of believers, effectively symbolizes and brings about the milieu of grace and forgiveness, of hope and loving communion.

—Jerome Theisen, OSB

Gathering the Nations

Let us preach the whole of God's plan to the powerful and to the humble, to rich and to poor, to men of every rank and age, as far as God gives us the strength, in season and out of season...

—St. Boniface

Bringing God's Justice

How do we make a ministry for justice and peace a constitutive dimension of monastic life? Some may think the question presumptuous, a putting of the cart before the horse. In other words, before I ask *how* monastic groups should be involved, shouldn't I ask *whether* they should be involved. I think the latter question is moot. If someone wants to write a book discussing whether or not monastic orders are exempt from the social teachings of the church, and, I might add, from the questions Christ said would be asked at the last Judgment, be my guest. I'm more old fashioned. I like the notion that the monastic community is a Church in miniature and, as such, has a responsibility to reflect on a smaller scale what the larger body can become.

—Mary Lou Kownacki, OSB

The Fight for Freedom

The story of African American Catholicism is the story of a people who obstinately clung to faith that gave them sustenance, even when it did not always make them welcome. Like many others, blacks had to fight for their faith; but their fight was often with members of their own household. Too long have black Catholics been anonymous. It is now clear that they can be identified, that their presence has made an impact, and that their contributions have made Catholicism a unique and stronger religious body.

—Cyprian Davis, OSB

Dialogue with World Religions

I have discovered that when you are in dialogue, an amazing phenomenon occurs: you share your faith and listen respectfully as the Buddhist, Hindu, Taoist or Muslim shares his or her heart's desire. What happens is that you begin to "feel" that what they are experiencing is the same as what you feel in your own heart. There is no need to correct one another's view; instead, there is a real and mutual acceptance of each other's way. You acknowledge to yourself that while their way may not be your way, you are bearing witness to the integrity of their way and it feels sound, good and true.

—Mary Margaret Funk, OSB

The Daily Manual Labor

Idleness is the enemy of the soul. Therefore, all the community must be occupied at definite times in manual labor and at other times in lectio divina.

—*Rule of St. Benedict* 48, § 1

The Work of Our Hands

Work is an integral part of all human life, be it inside or outside a monastery. What perhaps differentiates the monk's approach to work from that of his fellow humans is the attitude he brings to it. Monastery work is functional. It is not motivated by a desire for a career or for success, or even less by greed.

—Victor-Antoine D'Avila LaTourrette

Work and Prayer

Bodily work relieves pressures on the mind. Since the major symptom of the malady of *acedia* is that I am not able to pray anymore, work with my hands may help me be productive until my mind returns to concentration. My body restores rest to my overactive mind, and returns them to balance. Work is a back door to pure prayer. For a proficient practitioner, who is working mindfully, there is not distinction between work and prayer. Prayer is work and work is prayer.

—Mary Margaret Funk, OSB

Monastic Study

Only concentration on knowledge that is useful in life should be called study. There are two kinds: one is useful for acting and performing duties common to all humankind or those proper to one's profession; the other is useful for busying oneself honorably during leisure time and taking advantage of it, avoiding idleness and the vices it usually brings in its wake. The first goal should be action and the performance of our duties and obligations, both general and particular; the second, the good use of intervals in action when we are at leisure and at rest, a dangerous state for those not knowing how to use it well. But those who know how to take advantage of leisure time acquire during such intervals knowledge for self-fulfillment and for making themselves more fit for action, and they taste at the same time the innocent pleasure of relaxation.

—Jean Mabillon, OSB

Love of Learning and the Desire for God

(Gertrude the Great speaks of herself in the third person in the following revelation.)

Hence her love of learning now became desire for knowledge of God. Never tired of pondering over the pages of all the books of Holy Scripture that she was able to obtain or acquire, she filled the coffers of her heart to the brim with the sweetest and most useful sentences of Holy Scripture. And so she was always ready with godly and edifying words to help those who came to consult her and to refute errors with the testimony of Holy Scripture in such a way that no one could demolish her arguments. In those days she could never tire of the sweet pleasure she found in the contemplation of God and in the study of scripture, which was for her honey in the mouth (Ps 118:3; Rev 10:9, etc.), music in the ear, and spiritual jubilation in the heart.

—St. Gertrude the Great

Community of Love

We experience "being accepted" in a particular way when the Father's love comes to us through the attitudes of our brethren. The monk who in his community experiences an accepting love like this finds in it the strength and encouragement to accept himself, in a deep, peaceful act of radical obedience. Acceptance of his own being and make-up, with its strengths, weaknesses, flaws, and individuality, is a man's primary obedience to the Creator, and it is also the necessary foundation for acceptance of others in their differentness from himself. Because in Christ he is accepted, he can accept others; because in Christ he has been welcomed, he can welcome his neighbor.

—Daniel Rees and other members of the English
Benedictine Congregation

Caesar's Coin

What are the "things of God"? *We are*. When we were baptized (or ordained deacons or priests, or when we professed religious vows or exchanged the vows of marriage) we became God's property in a special way: God claimed us as belonging, no longer to ourselves, but as belonging to God. Traditional theology talks about this as the "sacramental seal," that indelible mark on our soul that sets us apart; even better, that action of God that pulls us out of our own little world and puts us in God's world; God's choice, on our behalf, that forever identifies us—much like a coin is identified by the image and inscription of its maker pressed down deep into it.

—Kurt Stasiak, OSB

Love's Peace

When we believe we are loved by God, we can relax as with a friend and let all aspects of ourselves be known. We can admit our mistakes and sins because we know we are accepted and acceptable. In true humility, we no longer need to think of ourselves as better than others, nor to pity ourselves because we are worse than others. What we know more surely is that we are nothing without God. We do not create our own goodness, nor do we earn God's love by our efforts. We can only receive that goodness and love, and let that be the energy that motivates our good actions. Embracing this truth is what humility is all about.

—Katherine Howard, OSB

One in Christ

For Benedict, everything is centered in this loving of Christ that has become our own loving and which establishes our identity as true Christians. He writes, "Your way of acting must be different from the world's way; the love of Christ must come before all else" (4:20–21). In other words, it is precisely in the way that Christ's loving has become the center of our being that we are distinguished from the world, from all those who have not known or accepted Christ in faith. Ultimately, it is the Father's love that finds expression in Christ and in all those who have come to know and appropriate that love because they are one with Christ.

—Demetrius Dumm, OSB

Total Giving

Another way of grasping this element of the excessive in Christ's life is to perceive that he was obliged to include within his brief life span every single thing that God needs in order to express himself. In the same way it appears exorbitant that the poverty expected of our own selves before we can start sharing in divine glory must be total and absolute.

—Abbot Denis Huerre, OSB

Light from Light

My soul, have you found what you are looking for? You were looking for God, and you have discovered that he is the supreme being, and that you could not possibly imagine anything more perfect. You have discovered that this supreme being is life itself, light wisdom, goodness, eternal blessedness and blessed eternity. He is everywhere, and he is timeless. Lord my God, you gave me life and restored it when I lost it. Tell my soul that so longs for you what else you are besides what it has already understood, so that it may see you clearly. It stands on tiptoe to see more, but apart from what it has seen already, it sees nothing but darkness. Of course it does not really see darkness, because there is no darkness in you, but it sees that it can see no further because of the darkness in itself. Surely, Lord, inaccessible light is your dwelling place, for no one apart from yourself can enter into it and fully comprehend you.

—St. Anselm

The Ladder of Humility

Any monk or nun who has climbed all these steps of humility will come quickly to that love of God which in its fullness casts out all fear. Carried forward by that love, they will begin to observe without effort as though naturally from good habit all those precepts which in earlier days were kept at least partly through fear.

—*Rule of St. Benedict* 7

Humility's Unfolding

Humility, Benedict teaches, treads tenderly upon the life around it. When we know our place in the universe, we can afford to value the place of others. We need them, in fact, to make up what is wanting in us. We stand in the face of others without having to take up all the space. We don't have to dominate conversations or consume all the time or call all the attention to ourselves. There is room, humility knows, for all of us in life. We are each an ember of the mind of God and we are each sent to illumine the other through the dark places of life to sanctuaries of truth and peace where God can be God for us because we have relieved ourselves of the ordeal of being God ourselves. We can simply unfold ourselves and become.

—Joan Chittister, OSB

A Time in the Desert

The Desert is silent.
Why was this unexpected?
Only the wind can call
where no life is,
and water fled.
Ravens high searching for carrion
give rare and distant voice,
but the still rocks speak no word
as they shimmer in the heat.

And yet the soul is summoned forth
to give answer clear enough
as the Sun's pitiless eye,
veiled by no cloud of the softly irrelevant,
sees straight to the ultimate question:
Whence is your being?
Who is your Master now?
The beasts of the Desert
are creatures of the night perforce.
For here the Moon is the only friend:
I saw her rise full
between the misty mountains,
drawing her silvery path
over the sulphurous waters
of that deepest desert
wherein the Jordan dies.

My life was turned:
I passed right through:
My tent is left behind.

—Philip Jebb, OSB

The Imitation of Christ

The imitation of our Lord consists not so much of basing our lives on an external model, but of lending ourselves with flexibility to the living influence of the Lord who is within us, in such a way that our activity is a continuous translation or expression of the life of the Lord within us. That is simply taking our part in what God has done for us and with us. If this were simply words, a concept, a manner of speech, you would be absolutely right to feel annoyed. Let the old man continue to live in you. Be yourself. It wasn't serious: just a formula, a system, a theory. But if this is true, if it is no longer I who live but Christ who lives in me, don't you see the nature of this imitation, don't you see the rigour of the concept? Don't distress yourself, don't try to escape from the words of the Lord: "Today if you will hear his voice, harden not your hearts" (Ps 94[95]:8). Voluntary inattention doesn't do away with reality, nor with our duty, nor with our responsibility before God. You belong to God. You do not belong to yourself. You have no right to split your life into two parts, one trying hard to be supernatural, and the other developing itself freely, at random, separated from God.

—Abbot Paul Delatte

Christ's Spirit

We also have as our Paraclete our Lord Jesus Christ. Although we are unable to see him bodily, we recollect what he did and taught in the body, as written down in the gospels. If we commit ourselves with all care to hearing, reading, conferring with one another, and preserving these [deeds and teachings] in heart and body, it is sure that we will easily overcome the hardships of this age—as if the Lord were sojourning with us forever and consoling us. If we love this Paraclete and keep his commandments, he will ask the Father, and he will give us another Paraclete—that is, he will in his clemency pour forth the grace of his Spirit into our hearts, and it will gladden us in the expectation of our heavenly homeland in the midst of the adversities of our present exile. Then we will be able to say with the prophet, *According to the multitude of my sorrows in my heart, your paraclesis, that is, your consolations, O Lord, have gladdened my soul.*

—Bede the Venerable

Waiting for the Bridegroom

Certainly Christ is indeed present to us all during the centuries of our Christian history, since he lives and we live by his life. But no less really is he absent, since he remains invisible and like a stranger to our sensible world. This permanent absence of Christ lays the foundation of the regular fast. Besides the feast days when the church recalls the meeting with Christ at Easter and anticipates the meeting at the Parousia, the whole of Christian time is marked by the remoteness of the Bridegroom, the wait for his coming, and consequently by fasting. The monk's habitual solitude is also added to this absence of Christ: the Lord's visits under the appearances of a guest only interrupt transiently a normal state of separation.

—Adalbert de Vogüé

The Meaning of Prayer

Prayer is what links the religious and the spiritual, the inner and the outer dimensions of life. Every spiritual tradition on earth forms a person in some kind of regular practice designed to focus the mind and the spirit. Regular prayer reminds us that life is punctuated by God, awash in God, encircled by God. To interrupt the day with prayer—with any centering activity that draws us beyond the present to the consciousness of eternal truth—is to remind ourselves of the timelessness of eternity. Prayer and regular spiritual practices serve as a link between this life and the next. They remind us of what we are doing and why we're doing it and where our lives are going. They give us the strength of heart to sustain us on the way. When life goes dry, only the memory of God makes life bearable again. Then we remember that whatever is has purpose.

—Joan Chittister, OSB

The Tools of Good Works

Don't get too involved in purely worldly affairs, and count nothing more important than the love you should cherish for Christ. Don't let your actions be governed by anger nor nurse your anger against a future opportunity of indulging it. Don't harbor in your heart any trace of deceit nor pretend to be at peace with another when you are not; don't abandon the true standards of charity. Don't use oaths to make your point for fear of perjury, but speak the truth with integrity of heart and tongue.

—*Rule of St. Benedict* 4

O Gracious Maker of the Stars

O gracious Maker of the Stars
That curb the darkness of the night,
To you we raise our humble prayers
And trust in your redeeming light.

For in your mercy grieved to see
Our world so torn by sin and death
You came on earth to touch our wounds
And heal us with your living breath.

The world was drifting on its way
To dark despair and deepening gloom
When calmly, as the Bridegroom comes,
You came from Mary's virgin womb.

Before your might, O gentle Lord,
May every creature bend the knee
And may the silent planets praise
The God who comes to set us free.

This evening keep us, holy Lord,
Within your presence all the while
That in your kingdom we may live
Forever safe from Satan's guile.

May power and praise and glory be
To God the Father and the Son
Who came on earth that we might be
Within the Spirit ever one.

—Trans. Ralph Wright, OSB

Seeking the Lord

Lord, if thou art not here, where shall I seek thee, being absent? But if thou art everywhere, why do I not see thee present? Truly thou dwellest in unapproachable light. But where is unapproachable light, or how shall I come to it? Or who shall lead me to that light and into it, that I may see thee in it? Again, by what marks, under what form, shall I seek thee? I have never seen thee, O Lord, my God; I do not know thy form. What, O most high Lord, shall this man do, an exile far from thee: What shall thy servant do, anxious in his love of thee, and cast out afar from thy face? He pants to see thee, and thy face is too far from him. He longs to come to thee, and thy dwelling-place is inaccessible. He is eager to find thee, and knows not thy place. He desires to see thee, and does not know thy face. Lord, thou art my God, and thou art my Lord, and never have I seen thee. It is thou that hast made me, and has made me anew, and hast bestowed upon me all the blessings I enjoy; and not yet do I know thee. Finally, I was created to see thee, and not yet have I done that for which I was made.

—St. Anselm

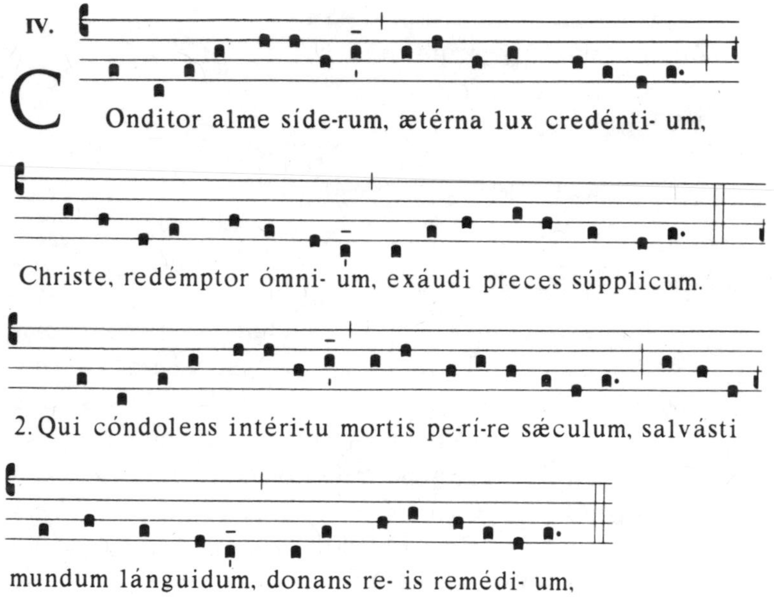

From *Liber Hymnarius,* ed. Benedictines of Solesmes, p. 3. Used by permission of les Editions de Solesmes, Abaye Saint-Pierre de Solesmes, Sablé-sur-Sarthe, France.

From Darkness to Light

The movement from darkness to light and back into darkness is the common rhythm of natural life and it is also a spiritual rhythm. God is a hidden God, both knowable and supremely unknowable. Movements of intellectual awareness are movements into the light, moments of intuitive awareness are movements into the dark. Often, long stretches of our life are seen as times of shadow, although subsequent examination shows that there were periods bathed in the glory of light.

—Paula Fairlie, OSB

Silence

In a monastery we ought to follow the advice of the psalm which says: I have resolved to keep watch over my ways so that I may not sin with my tongue. I am guarded about the way I speak and have accepted silence in humility, refraining even from words that are good [Ps 39: 2–3]. In this verse the psalmist shows that, because of the value of silence, there are times when it is best not to speak even though what we have in mind is good. How much more important it is to refrain from evil speech when we remember what such sins bring down on us in punishment. In fact, so important is it to cultivate silence, even about matters concerning sacred values and spiritual instruction, that permission to speak should be granted only rarely to monks and nuns, even though they may themselves have achieved a high standard of monastic observance. After all, it is written in scripture that one who never stops talking cannot avoid falling into sin [Prov 10:19]. Another text in the same book reminds us that the tongue holds the key to death and life [Prov 18:21]. We should remember that speaking and instructing belong to the teacher; the disciple's role is to be silent and listen.

—*Rule of St. Benedict* 6

Listening for a Word

Silence and listening and hearing and obedience, then, require trust—trust that God wants to speak a word to me, trust that God *has* a particular will for me, trust that God's will for me is always good even if I cannot yet see its goodness for me, trust that God *does* speak through some whom he calls to a special leadership, trust that my obedience even to a mistaken judgment by another will make me a better listener and a less self-willed disciple, trust that God will make a better good come from my obedience even if the abbot's direction is wrong-headed.

—Mark O'Keefe, OSB

A New Song

The listening, which can go on all day amid a variety of occupations, is concentrated when we give up time to be alone with God in prayer. Prayer is an exposure to the reality of God. For those who pray regularly the time may come fairly soon when particular thoughts or words no longer seem to help. Prayer seems to have gone dead. The relationship is moving into a new phase, and you have to learn to change gear.

—Maria Boulding, OSB

The Road Unseen

It is so easy for us to make out a little programme of the spiritual life for ourselves, quite nicely constructed according to our capabilities, our aptitudes, the means we have to hand, etc., and so, pleasantly, happily, we would end up living a nice honest little life. But the Lord passes, and with a single gesture brushes aside this construction, which was harmless, but which would have led us only to mediocrity; and, instead of allowing us to be an expounder of beautiful theories on the spiritual life, detachment, self-denial, he arranges things in such a way as to make us practice them. That is how saints are made. No one ever arrived at sanctity except by that complete and absolute overturning of their projects, their plans, their arrangements. The remarkable thing about the religious life is that, unless we actually break our vows, we become saints either willingly or by force.

—Abbess Cécile Bruyère, OSB

A Prayer to Make a Difference

O Lord, help me know your will for me. Let your light shine in the depth of my heart that I may know what you want me to do with my life. Help me believe that you have a special plan for me. Lord, I know I pass through this life only once; help me decide how you want me to make a difference. Like your Blessed Mother, give me the wisdom to hear your voice and the courage to answer your call. Above all give me peace of mind and heart. I offer this prayer in your name. Amen.

—Archbishop Daniel M. Buechlein, OSB

The Time Is Now

Now is the hour for us to rise from sleep! St. Paul (from whom these words were taken) and the Christians of his time were under the impression that the *parousia,* the return of Christ in glory, was about to happen and they, therefore, frequently encouraged one another to "wake up" or "stay awake!" However, as the Lord did not return, those Christians, while remaining hopeful, had to learn to live within the confines of this often unsupportive world. St. Benedict, while also looking forward to a life which is to come, exhorted his disciples to arise from sleep but his intention was that they might, thereby, see the coming of the Lord in a number of quite ordinary ways. He comes, according to the Rule, in people whom we meet, in Scripture which we can take up and read and in the intimacy of our quiet, private prayer!

—Ambrose Tinsely, OSB

True Prayer

We must be quite clear that our prayer will be heard, not because of the eloquence and length of all we have to say, but because of our heartfelt repentance and openness of heart to the Lord whom we approach. Our prayer should, therefore, be free from all other preoccupations and it should normally be short, although we may well on occasions be inspired to stay longer in prayer through the gift of God's grace working within us. Our prayer together in community, on the other hand, should always be moderate in length, and when the sign is given by the superior, all should rise together.

—*Rule of St. Benedict* 20

All Saints Hymn

Rejoice with all the saints this day,
Who ran by faith the narrow way.
The great and low together stand
With glory crowned at God's right hand.

How blest are they the Spirit's poor,
Their king is Jesus Christ the Lord,
And all who mourned have found new birth;
The patient meek await the earth.

How blest are those who fought the fight,
God's justice fills their thirst for right.
The pure of heart God's face behold;
The merciful have overflowed.

How blest are those who wrought the peace
As heirs they share the Victor's feast;
And prophets by injustice slain
Have claimed the Kingdom's righteous reign.

Come martyrs red and virgins white,
All teachers wise and students bright,
All wives and husbands, monks and nuns,
With bishops, priests, and deacons, come.

Come holy men and women all
With heart and voice sing praise and call
To Christ who rose triumphantly
That we may join your company.

Most blest the Father and the Son.
Most blest the Spirit, Three in One.
Your Kingdom come, your will be done.
Your praise forever more be sung. Amen.

—Harry Hagan, OSB

Divine Excess

Carried away one day by the excess of her love, she said to the Lord: "Would, O Lord, that I might have a fire that could liquefy my soul so that I could pour it totally out like a libation unto thee!" The Lord answered: "Thy will is such a fire."

—St. Gertrude the Great

Mother of Comfort

O sovereign Lady...I have experienced the constancy of your mercies so many times! In fact, with your help I have so often escaped the captivity of my sin that it would perhaps be better not to speak of my "former" enslavements when there have been so many deliveries from captivity. When repeated sinning produces a cruel hardening of my heart, an immediate, almost instinctive return to you mollifies me; and when I consider the misery within me and am about to sink into despair, I feel in my unhappy soul, whether I like it or not, a renewed assurance that I will be drawn toward you. Thus I am convinced that whatever bad things I am involved in, you owe it to me, if I dare say so, not to fail me if I am in need. I have been cast into your arms since I left my mother's womb; if you were not to come after me when I turn away, if you were to reject me when I come back to you, you would be the one I would justly blame for my perdition. But since it is well known that the Son's power reverberates in the Mother, from whom could I better solicit my salvation than from you? Sharing the condition of servant with you, I can cry out: "I am thine!" [Ps 119:94].

—Guibert of Nogent

God Alone

And when prayer is come to perfection, then will the soul also mount to the supreme degree of Humility, which regards God considered absolutely in Himself, and without any express or distinct comparison with creatures; for hereby a soul fixing her sight upon God as all in all, and contemplating Him in the darkness of incomprehensibility, does not by any distinct act or reflection consider the vacuity and nothingness of creatures, but really transcends and forgets them, so that to her they are in very deed as nothing, because they are not the object which with her spirit she only sees, and with her affections only embraces.

—Augustin Baker, OSB

Heart and Soul

Lord! Now am I a naked soul and thou a God most glorious! Our twofold intercourse is love eternal which can never die. Now comes a blessed stillness welcome to both. He gives himself to her and she to him. What shall now befall her, the soul knows: therefore am I comforted. Where two lovers come secretly together, they must often part, without parting.

—Mechthild of Magdeburg

God's Coming

Jesus is thrice-born. Christian tradition honors his human birth at Bethlehem as a visible event between two invisible births: his eternal birth as Son of the Father in the splendors of the Trinity, and his birth by grace in the life of every human being who accepts him. All three of the births are real, but not all are historical. His Trinitarian birth as the

Father's Word is outside history, in the eternal Now of God's life. His human birth of Mary, from the stock of Israel, is an event in historical time, more or less datable. His hidden birth in people's lives takes place again and again, and will continue through all the time of human history.

—Maria Boulding, OSB

Sequence for the Virgin

A royal scepter and a crown
of purple, a fortress
strong as mail! O fortress
of maidenhood, scepter
all verdant:

The way you bloomed would have startled
the grandsire of us all,
for the life father Adam
stripped from his sons (praise
to you!) slid from your loins.

You never sprang from the dew,
my blossom, nor from the rain—
that was no wind that swept
over you—for God's
radiance opened you
on a regal bough. On the morn

of the universe he saw you
blossoming, and he made you
a golden matrix, O maid
beyond praise, for his word.

Strong rib of Adam! Out of you
God sculpted woman: the mirror

of all his charms, the caress
of his whole creation. So voices

chime in heaven and the whole
earth marvels at Mary,
beloved beyond measure.

Cry, aloud! A serpent
hissed and a sea of grief
seeped through his forked
words into woman. The mother

of us all miscarried.
With ignorant hands she
plucked at her womb and bore
woe without bounds.

But the sunrise from your thighs
burnt the whole of her guilt away.
More than all that Eve lost
is the blessing you won.

Mary, savior,
mother of light:
may the limbs of your son be the chords of the song
the angels chant above.

—Hildegard of Bingen

Surrender

To bear sickness, pain, poverty, is a simple matter; I mean that it may be very hard, and need great heroism, but it is simple, straightforward and obvious, and therefore easy (in one sense). Just as it is easy to walk twenty miles, but difficult to drive a motor twenty miles, though the former is far more tiring. So it is less painful (sometimes) to bear spiritual discomfort, but it is much more difficult to do—or rather, more difficult to know how—because it is not simple, straightforward and obvious. But when once you know how, it is quite simple; just as a chauffeur, who drives daily, does it automatically and unconsciously. Now the way is this: accept with simplicity, or (better) take and seize with both hands, whatever feelings God sends you.

—John Chapman, OSB

Compassion for the Sick

The care of those in the community who are sick is an absolute priority which must rank before every other requirement, so that there may be no doubt that it is Christ who is truly served in them. After all, Christ himself said: I was sick and you came to visit me, and also: What you did to one of these my least brethren you did to me [Matt 25: 36–40]. The sick themselves, on the other hand, should remember that the care and attention they receive is offered them to show honor to God, and so they must be careful not to distress by selfish and unreasonable demands those attending to their needs. Still such behavior in the sick should be tolerated by those attending them, who will receive a richer reward for their patience. The abbot or abbess should certainly make very sure that the sick suffer no neglect.

—*Rule of St. Benedict* 36

We Watch for You, O Lord, till Break of Day

We watch for you, O Lord, till break of day,
Through all the long, cold darkness of our pain.
We yearn to see your face and hear you say
That nothing we have suffered is in vain.

We grieve the doubts that sat beside us here
And found us willing to believe them true
When we were deaf to every voice but fear
That questioned all the hope we had of you.

We sorrow at the selfish ways we chose
To disregard the message of the cross,
As we forgot, so quickly, that you rose
And turned to gain what seemed to be death's loss.

We ask you pardon for our blinded eyes
And for the sullen prayers we hardly said
And for the stubborn pride that would not rise
And leave our place among the living dead.

Your love is wider than our narrow hearts,
Your pardon greater than our power to mourn.
Speak once again those words, like fiery darts,
That call us to come forth and be reborn!

—Genevieve Glen, OSB

Patient Endurance

The Scriptures reassure us: let your understanding strengthen your patience. In serenity look forward to the joy that follows sadness. Hope leads you to that joy and love enkindles your zeal. The well-prepared mind forgets the suffering inflicted from without and guides eagerly to what it has contemplated within itself.

—St. Peter Damian

Blessed Are the Pure of Heart

This is real inner poverty, the daily need to be converted and begin again; but it is also real security, the security in love we need if we are to be open to change, free enough in heart to let go of anything, anything at all, when the Spirit calls us on. The spirit who makes us cry "Abba" is not a child's comforter. He brings us to the brink of the abyss of love where we are asked, Do you *dare* to have nothing but the Father's love? This is what being a child of God is all about, the communion which is a sharing in Christ's Easter experience. You are being invited to be unshielded against the Father's love. You are not to have any insurance policy against the living God.

—Maria Boulding, OSB

The Regal Dark Mysterious Cross

The regal dark mysterious cross
In song is lifted high,
The wood on which our God was raised
As Man against the sky.

Upon this wood his body bore
The nails, the taunts, the spear,
Till water flowed with blood to wash
The whole world free of fear.

At last the song that David sung
Is heard and understood:
"Before the nations God as King
Reigns from his throne of wood."

This wood now spread with purple wears
The pageantry of kings;

Of chosen stock it dares to hold
   On high his tortured limbs.

O blessed Tree, upon whose arms
   The world's own ransom hung;
His body pays our debt and life
   From Satan's grasp is wrung.

O sacred Cross, our steadfast hope
   In this our Passiontide,
   Through you the Son obtained for all
   Forgiveness as he died.

May every living creature praise
   Our God both one and three,
   Who rules in everlasting peace
   All whom his cross makes free.

—Trans. Ralph Wright, OSB

Wondrous Love

The cross prompts two kinds of feeling in me. The first is incomprehension. How could God allow Jesus to come to such a cruel end on the cross? Although I know that it was human beings who nailed Jesus to the cross, there remains the provocation, the harshness, and incomprehensible nature of this death. It raises questions about my image of God and my image of Jesus. The other feeling is one of being filled with love. When I look at Jesus hanging on the cross with outstretched arms and dying there, I feel that I'm loved unconditionally. In the depth of my heart I know that in the end Jesus also died for me. He held nothing back. On the cross he gave everything, he opened himself for me. His outstretched arms are an invitation to me to feel secure in his love. When I kneel before the cross all self-accusations cease, and my heart becomes still. I know that all is well. Everything is embraced by his love.

—Anselm Grün

By His Wounds We Are Healed

I thought attentively of these things, when I perceived that the grace that I had so long asked by the aforesaid prayer was granted to me, unworthy though I am; for I perceived in spirit that Thou hadst imprinted in the depths of my heart the adorable marks of Thy sacred Wounds, even as they are on Thy Body; that Thou hadst cured my soul in imprinting these Wounds on it; and that, to satisfy its thirst, Thou hadst given it the precious beverage of Thy love.

—St. Gertrude the Great

Let Us Boast Not in Foolishness

Let us boast not in foolishness
But in the cross of Jesus Christ,
Who ransomed us from faithlessness
With his own blood as purchase price.

When ruthless enemies arose,
He came in love to take our part;
To foil the plotting of our foes
He sacrificed with willing heart.

O Lamb of God, we sing your praise
With Father and with Spirit blest.
Grant us to serve you all our days
And dwell with you in endless rest.

—Genevieve Glen, OSB

Christ in the Rubble

Genevieve Glen, OSB

For the dead and the bereaved, for the rescuers, and for the world
September 11, 2001

SEPTEMBER HOPE
Tobias Colgan, OSB

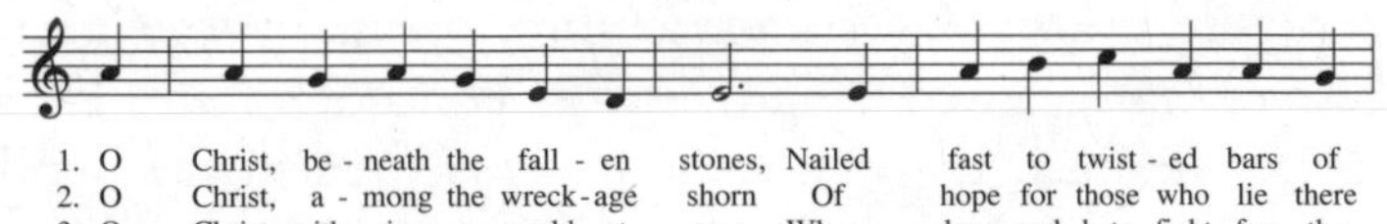

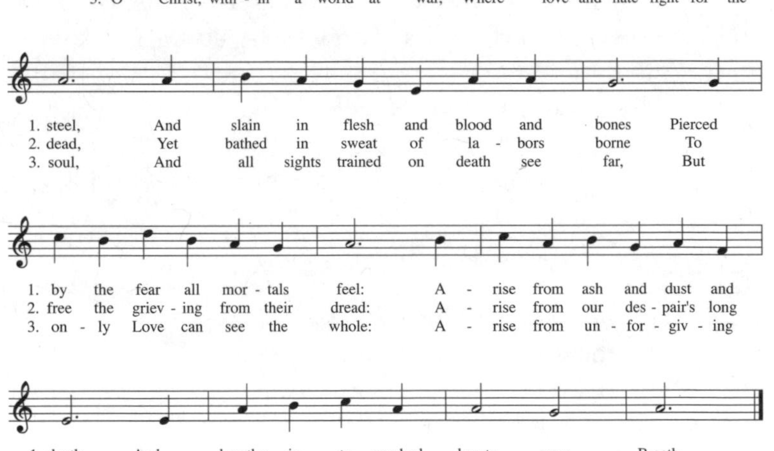

1. death, And breathe in - to crushed hearts new Breath.
2. night And pour up - on us liv - ing Light.
3. pain And teach us how to love a - gain.

Good Zeal

It is easy to recognize the bitter spirit of wickedness which creates a barrier to God's grace and opens the way to the evil of hell. But equally there is a good spirit which frees us from evil ways and brings us closer to God and eternal life. It is this latter spirit that all who follow the monastic way of life should strive to cultivate, spurred on by fervent love. By following this path, they try to be first to show respect to one another, with the greatest patience in tolerating weaknesses of body or character. They should even be ready to outdo each other in mutual obedience, so that no one in the monastery aims at personal advantage but is rather concerned for the good of others. Thus, the pure love of one another as belonging to one family should be their ideal. As for God, they should fear him with deep reverence. They should love their abbot or abbess with sincere and unassuming affection.

—*Rule of St. Benedict* 72

Holy Thursday

This is a night without words.
We only have memory.
Tomorrow we will lie flat on the ground because
without Christ there is, in the end, nothing left to
say.
So we are in the midst of a cloud of remembrance,
which has settled on all of us here:
God's Angel, Jesus, who, instead of taking flight
washed our feet first with water and then with his
own blood.
This is a night of golden memory when the bread and
the cup were forever transformed,

transfixed and transubstantiated into our divine
manna for our journey
through the desert.
This is a memorial of the act of divine humility
that asks only that we do the same.
What we do is in remembrance of him who
remembered us into this moment.
Let us sit down with him now and eat.
Without words.
With only gratitude for what must remain the silence
of God's unfathomable,
unconquerable love.

—Guerric DeBona, OSB

A Living Remembrance of the Lord

When the Apostles received the power and the command to change bread and wine into the Body and Blood of Christ, their commission was to have unlimited application and importance. It was not for themselves alone that they were to exercise this power and fulfill this command. They were to act in the name of Christ so that through them the action of Christ might be brought within the reach of all the people of all times. It is therefore the real action of Christ Himself that takes place in the mass; and it takes place there so that all the people of all times may have the opportunity of joining themselves to this action and of partaking of Christ's Body and Blood.

—Virgil Michel, OSB, and Basil Stegmann, OSB

A Living Sacrifice of Praise

In the Eucharistic celebration itself many elements express the divine nature of the ecclesial reality which is occurring; indeed, these elements are the very means of embodying and ensuring the particular and precise nature of what is happening; namely, that Christ is acting and that the community is entirely defined and comes into being only through what he does and accomplishes. Thus, for example, in the person of the bishop or priest Christ is represented as the head of this assembly. It is he who gathers it; it is under his authority that it stands; it is his word which is gratefully heard and pondered; it is together with him that the community will dare to speak a word back to the Father and make its thanksgiving offering to him.

—Jeremy Driscoll, OSB

Come to Me

To come to Christ is to come to the Lord, to come to the King, to the light, the fire, the bread, the vine, yes, and to life itself. You seek liberty? Come to the Lord. You seek security? Come to the King...Glory? Come to the light. You seek resurrection? Come to that which is life itself.

—Peter of Celle

The Effects of Liturgical Prayer

After the liturgy has held its disciples in a vivifying and intimate contact with the priesthood of Jesus Christ, after it has taught them to perform all the liturgical acts, Mass, Breviary, administration of the sacraments, etc., in a spirit of prayer, after securing these two primary and essential results of its method, it has a further salutary influence to exercise on this interior activity of the soul that in the silence of mental prayer strives for a more intimate union with its God. Indeed, we believe that the soul formed in liturgical prayer will possess a facility of communion with Heaven, a pliancy and fervor, which will make its hours of prayer more spontaneous and more sweet.

—Lambert Beauduin, OSB

In the Presence of the Angels

God is present everywhere—present to the good and to the evil as well, so that nothing anyone does escapes his notice [Prov 15:30]; that is the firm conviction of our faith. Let us be very sure, however, without a moment's doubt, that his presence to us is never so strong as while we are celebrating the work of God in the oratory. And so we should always recall at such times the words of the psalm: Serve the Lord with awe and reverence [Ps 2:11], and: Sing the Lord's praises with skill and relish [Ps 47:7], and: I shall sing your praise in the presence of the angels [Ps 138:1]. All of us, then, should reflect seriously on how to appear before the majesty of God in the presence of his angels. That will make sure that, when we sing in choir, there is complete harmony between the thoughts in our mind and the meaning of the words we sing.

—*Rule of St. Benedict* 19

Exiles in the House of God

The worship of the living God cannot be contained in any one place; and yet the beauty of material things in a place of worship gives color and voice and texture to the presence of God. This marriage of the material and the spiritual is part of the tradition of our Catholic faith. It makes real for each generation the truth of the Incarnation: God stepped into our world, and made himself at home. Beauty is the bay window through which we can look and see God at home....Our worship of God must necessarily move through the beautiful things of creation to enter the realm of the spirit, because God wants our inmost hearts, not just our outer senses. So, in a way, we will always be something of an exile in the present world. As lovely as it may be, it's not our final home, and worshipping God in spirit and truth always leaves us aware that there is more than what meets the eye.

—Archabbot Justin Duvall, OSB

Mysterium Tremendum

When material civilization had collapsed and the light of culture was almost extinguished, then it was that men turned to that mystery of truth which lies beyond the material world and beyond all human wisdom. They had the Bible, they had the commentaries of the Fathers of the Church, and they had some remains of classical learning, which were preserved in the monasteries. It was from these sources that their contemplation was fed: it was from them that the great structure of the sacred liturgy was built up. We have grown so accustomed to the idea that the material world and human history are the proper object of human study that we find it difficult to understand a world in which these studies played so little part. To the medieval man the supreme event in human history, which transcended all the wonders of the material world, was the incarnation of the Son of God.

—Bede Griffiths

The Word in Worship

God has revealed Himself not only as Father, but also as the *Logos,* the Word. This revelation, too, must have deep significance for our Christian life. *Logos* means *word.* From all eternity, the Second Person of the Trinity infinitely "speaks" the greatness, the beauty, the goodness, the truth of the Father. Hence St. Paul could say: Christ is the *"Amen"* to the Father. But He needs no "words" with which to speak. His entire infinite Personality is in Itself an infinitely eloquent *yes* to the Father as truth, as beauty, as goodness. We might say that from all eternity the word is the "praise" of the Father. And since it was the *Logos,* the Word, who became man, and by baptism has made us His members and His brothers, does it not follow that our first and chiefest obligations as sons of God and brothers of Christ—in fact that our *total* obligation, which includes all else—is that we also "praise" the Father? That we say "yes" to Him by worship?

—Godfrey Diekmann, OSB

Unity in Diversity

And so, we assemble. We come together as an identifiable group of people who, in spite of differences that may be profound and acute, share a common conviction that Jesus is central to the meaning and goal of human existence. The very fact that in this pluralistic world in which people are told they are free to go their own way, to do their own thing, to be themselves, we nonetheless come together to profess a common faith in the lordship of Jesus and perform a common action of offering thanks and sharing in a ritual meal is a remarkable phenomenon, becoming more and more remarkable as society gives evidence of becoming more and more fragmented.

—William Skudlarek, OSB

Liturgical Action

It is not only the faithful whose faith is reanimated by the liturgy. The indifferent, even the adversaries in spite of themselves, feel the influence of this externalized religious life. The grand cathedrals, inspired by the liturgy and constructed for it, and rising in our public places; the towers, cupolas, spires, symbols of our faith, which catch the eye from a distance and dominate our public dwellings and our private residences; the chimes, which sing out; the processions that take place; the funeral corteges that pray and hope; the joyful crowds that go in long files to the house of the Lord to celebrate our grand religious solemnities; the liturgical cycle, sending its rhythm into the civil life and imposing on the latter respect for its holy days—in a word, all the exterior manifestations that the liturgy inspires, animates, and preserves, are a protest against this atheistic secularization, and constitute in our midst *a constant affirmation of the supernatural and of the rights of God.*

—Lambert Beauduin, OSB

Preaching in Love

So who am I to be a watchman, for I do not stand on the mountain of action but lie down in the valley of weakness? Truly the all-powerful Creator and Redeemer of mankind can give me in spite of my weaknesses a higher life and effective speech; because I love him, I do not spare myself in speaking of him.

—Gregory the Great

The Divine Cloud

It is only by degrees that the soul is efficaciously enabled by the Divine Spirit to ascend above the imagination, and to dwell habitually in a higher sphere, free from encumbrance. If, when she has reached this clearer sphere, she have need of any particular images for some business which requires their use, then she calls for them, and awakes them in the imagination, where they lie dormant, and up they come to serve her turn. When she has done with them she bids them go to sleep again, in the imagination, till she may have further need for them, and they, like the centurion's servants in the Gospel, come and go at her bidding. Thus she keeps down all affairs of this life, and all other images, under the cloud of forgetting, and, transcending them, she habitually turns her eyes upwards to that dark Cloud of Unknowing which is between her and her God.

—Augustin Baker, OSB

The Spirit within Us

When you are before God in prayer, you are consenting to his creation of you in the depths of your being, consenting precisely to his creation in you of the relationship we call "prayer." He creates in you the longing for union with him because it is first his longing. Your existence is his word of love; your desire for him is acquiescence in the love that loved first. Your "naked intent unto God" unleashes in you the creative Spirit of whom you are only partially aware, somewhat in the same way that the celebration of the sacraments in faith unleashes in you the dynamism of the paschal mystery, the dying and being reborn.

—Maria Boulding, OSB

A Taste for Prayer

The desire for prayer is that internal attraction towards prayer. It is not a question of our attitude being "I ought to pray," but a question of "I want to pray." It is true there is a midway stage where I can say, "I want to do what I ought to do." And this is fair and proper, but it is insufficient.

There has to grow with us a desire for prayer, a nostalgia for prayer, a taste for prayer....But the desire for prayer is something which comes, I suspect, only slowly and with practice. I think it is a truism of prayer to say that the desire for it, the taste for it, follows the practice of it. It is not because we are drawn to prayer that we first begin to pray; more often we have to begin prayer, and then the taste and the desire for it come.

—Cardinal Basil Hume, OSB

Still Waters Run Deep

It is because this kingdom is established and is present within us that we can be made free of the limitations of language and thought. Our attempt to achieve this silence may be difficult. It will almost certainly be prolonged. It is not just a matter of keeping our tongues still but much more of achieving a state of alert stillness in our mind and heart, which is not a state of consciousness familiar to most Westerners. We tend either to be alert or relaxed; rarely are the two states combined in most of us. But in meditation we come to experience ourselves as at one and the same time totally relaxed and totally alert. This stillness is not the stillness of sleep but rather of totally awakened concentration.

—John Main, OSB

Longing for God

There are many kinds of contemplation in which the soul devoted to Thee, O Christ, takes its delight, but in none of these do I so rejoice as in that which, ignoring all things, directs a simple glance of the untroubled spirit to Thee alone, O God. What peace and rest and joy does the soul find in Thee then....The heart burns within, the spirit rejoices, the memory grows fresh, the intellect clear, and the whole spirit, on fire with longing for the vision of Thy beauty, sees itself carried away to the love of those things which are invisible.

—John of Fécamp

How God Serves Us

My Lord,

I thank you that you have taken all earthly riches from me, for since then, you have clothed and fed me through the goodness of others. Because of this, I no longer can clothe my heart in the pride of possessing such things....I pray too for all those of pure heart who gave up everything for the Love of God. We are all arch-beggers who shall be judged on the last day by Jesus, our Redeemer and Lord. Change in me all that I lament in your presence and all that I lament in all sinners. All that I ask, I pray you to grant to me and to all imperfect spiritual people for your own glory. Your praise, O Lord, shall never be silent in my heart, no matter what I do or suffer or leave undone.

—Mechthild of Magdeburg

Vision of Light

On the feast of the blessed apostle James, while I was in a trance and seeing a vision of the ways of God, I was lifted up into the height and contemplated the mountain of God as if from nearby. And behold that immense light that abides on the summit of the mountain seemed to be cut through the center. I looked through it and saw a multitude of saints whose number I could not guess. My guide said to me, "Look and see and examine all those whom you see. Here you see holy martyrs, bishops and confessors of the Lord, monastic virgins of both sexes, widows and secular people, both married and chaste, those of high birth and of low, all reigning with Christ. They walked in the ways of the Lord, the holy paths that you have seen, and they arrived and received the unfading grace from Christ the Lord with His angels. Let all now contemplate their own path: If they walk on it unjustly, let them correct themselves with humility and charity and obedience and make straight their way. Because if they arrive, they will receive the eternal reward."

—Elisabeth of Schönau

Come, O Spirit, Holy One

Come, O Spirit, Holy One,
Into earth's great darkness come
With a beam of heaven's light.

Father of the poor, O come!
Giver of all gifts, O come!
Light of every contrite heart.

Great Consoler, loved-for Guest,
To our turbulence bring rest
Make your home in every soul.

Bring your cool to summer's heat,
To our toil bring your relief,
With your balm heal every grief.

Blessed Light, O kindle fire!
Make our wayward hearts that tire
Radiant with your own desire.

Distanced from your gifts of grace,
Man becomes a desert waste—
Nothing in him to bring peace.

Cleanse what sin has left defiled.
Water what is parched or dry.
Heal the wounded, sick or tired.

Bend the proud and stubborn mind.
Warm what sin keeps cold or bound.
Help the lost the road to find.

Grant to all who do believe
Through your grace in seven streams
Hope and strength for every need.

Grant us power to do your will.
Keep us safe till all is well.
Grant a joy that none can tell.

—Trans. Ralph Wright, OSB

Blessed Trinity in One

As the Flame of a fire has three qualities, so there is one God in three Persons. How? A flame is made up of brilliant light and red power and fiery heat. It has brilliant light that it may shine, and red power that it may endure, and fiery heat that it may burn. Therefore, by the brilliant light understand the Father, who with paternal love opens His brightness to His faithful; and by the red power, which is in the flame that it may be strong, understand the Son, Who took on a body born from a Virgin, in which His divine wonders were shown; and by the fiery heat understand the Holy Spirit, who burns ardently in the minds of the faithful.

—Hildegard of Bingen

Life Ablaze

God of truth and God of beauty, seed in us, as in Hildegard, a knowledge of good and evil, so that knowing one from the other, we may grow in passion for good and in awareness of evil. Give us the mind to bring knowledge to others and the heart to say the truth under all circumstances. Give us a love for the intellectual life and the stamina to pursue it so that, filled with your truth, we may never become enamored of anything less in life.

—Joan Chittister, OSB

The Desire for God

This mystery of love becomes itself a matter for reflection; its accomplishment demands our understanding its exigencies and its foundations. Thus it is the whole work of grace in us that we must consider. This opens up perspectives on the whole domain of what we must do for God...

—Jean Leclercq, OSB

Only a Beginning

They should value nothing whatever above Christ himself, and may he bring us all together to eternal life.

—*Rule of St. Benedict* 72

SANCTI
BENEDICTI

Sources

Anselm. "Proslogium," in *The Liturgy of The Hours*, vol. 2 (New York: Catholic Book Publishing, 1976), 1774.

______. "Proslogium," in *The Fire and the Cloud: An Anthology of Catholic Spirituality*, edited by David A. Fleming, SM (New York/Toronto/Ramsey: Paulist Press, 1978), 79.

Baker, OSB, Augustin. *Holy Wisdom or Directions for the Prayer of Contemplation* (London: Burns, Oates and Washbourne, 1876), 317.

______."Preface," from *The Divine Cloud*, edited by Henry Collins (London: Thomas Richardson and Son, 1971), xi–xii.

Beauduin, OSB, Lambert. *Liturgy: The Life of the Church*, translated by Virgil Michel, OSB (Collegeville, MN: Liturgical Press, 1929), 86–87, 28–29.

Bede the Venerable. *Homilies on the Gospels, Book II*, translated by Lawrence T. Marten and David Hurst, OSB (Kalamazooo, MI: Cistercian Publications, 1991), 165–66.

Boniface. "Letter," in *The Liturgy of The Hours*, vol. 3 (New York: Catholic Book Publishing, 1976), 1457.

Boulding, Maria. *The Coming of God* (Conception, MO: The Printery House, 2000), 105, 82, 49, 83.

______. "A Tapestry, from the Wrong Side," in *A Touch of God: Eight Monastic Journeys*, edited by Maria Boulding (Still River, MA: St. Bede's, 1983), 39–40.

Bruyère, OSB, Cécile. "Letter," 11 January 1891, in *The Spirit of Solesmes: The Christian Life in the Works of Dom Prosper Guéranger, Abbess Cécile Bruyère and Dom Paul Delatte,* edited by Sister Mary David Totah, OSB (Petersham, MA: St. Bede Publications, 1997), 76.

Buechlein, OSB, Archbishop Daniel M. "A Prayer to Make a Difference" (Indianapolis, IN: Vocations Office, 2000).

Chapman, OSB, John. *The Spiritual Letters of Dom John Chapman, OSB,* edited by Dom Roger Hudleston, OSB (London: Sheed and Ward, 1935), 42.

Chittister, OSB, Joan. *Rule of Benedict: Insights for the Ages* (New York: Crossroads, 1993), 72–73.

———. *Called to Question* (Lanham, MD: Sheed & Ward, 2004), 44.

———. *Life Ablaze: A Woman's Novena* (Eric, PA: Benetvision, 1997), 23.

Davis, OSB, Cyprian. *The History of Black Catholics in the United States* (New York: Orbis, 1990), 259.

DeBona, OSB, Guerric. "O, Happy Fault." Homily for The Easter Vigil, Year B in *Lift Up Your Hearts* (New York/Mahwah, NJ: Paulist Press, 2005), 94.

Delatte, OSB, Paul. "Retreat, 1909," in *The Spirit of Solesmes: The Christian Life in the Works of Dom Prosper Guéranger, Abbess Cécile Bruyère and Dom Paul Delatte,* edited by Sister Mary David Totah, OSB (Petersham, MA: St. Bede Publications, 1997), 58–59.

Diekmann, OSB, Godfrey. *Come, Let Us Worship* (Baltimore, MD: Helicon Press, 1961), 73.

Driscoll, OSB, Jeremy. *Theology at the Eucharistic Table: Master Themes in the Theological Tradition* (Rome and Leominster, UK: Centro Studi S. Anselmo and Gracewing Publishing, 2003), 16.

Dumm, OSB, Demetrius. *Cherish Christ Above All: The Bible in the Rule of Benedict* (New York/Mahwah, NJ: Paulist Press, 1996), 51.

DuVall, OSB, Justin. Homily for the Dedication of the Church of the Monastery of the Immaculate Conception, Ferdinand, Indiana, used with permission of the author.

Elisabeth of Schönau. *The Complete Works,* translated by Anne L. Clark (New York/Mahwah, NJ: Paulist Press, 2000), 166–67.

Fairlie, OSB, Paula. "Foreshadowings," in *A Touch of God: Eight Monastic Journeys,* edited by Maria Boulding (Still River, MA: St. Bede's, 1983), 97.

Funk, OSB, Mary Margaret. *Thoughts Matter: The Practice of Spiritual Life* (New York: Continuum, 1998), 101.

______. *Islam I…: An Experience of Dialogue and Devotion* (New York: Lantern, 2003), 17–18.

Gertrude the Great. "Spiritual Exercises," in *The Flowing Light of the Godhead,* in *The Fire and The Cloud: An Anthology of Catholic Spirituality,* edited by David A. Fleming, SM (New York/Toronto/Ramsey, NJ: Paulist Press, 1978), 96.

______. "The Life and Revelation of Saint Gertrude the Great," in *An Anthology of Christian Mysticism,* edited by Harvey Egan, SJ (Collegeville, MN: Liturgical Press, 1991), 260.

Glen, OSB, Genevieve. *Voices from the Valley: Hymn Texts with Biblical Reflections* (NE Hassalo, OR: OCP, 2003), 73, 41.

Gregory the Great. "Homily on Ezekiel," in *The Liturgy of The Hours,* vol. 4 (New York: Catholic Book Publishing, 1976), 1365–66.

Griffiths, Bede. *The Golden String* (Springfield, IL: Templegate, 1980), 157.

Grün, Anselm. *Images of Jesus,* translated by John Bowden (New York and London: Continuum, 2002), 147–48.

Guibert of Nogent. *A Monk's Confession: The Memoirs of Guibert of Nogent,* translated by Paul J. Archambault (University Park, PA: Pennsylvania State UP, 1996), 12–13.

Hagan, OSB, Harry. "My Choice," published with permission of the author.

______. "All Saints Hymn" (Portland, OR: OCP Publications, 2001).

Harris, OSB, Kym. "Perseverance," in the *Benedictine Handbook* (Collegeville, MN: Liturgical Press, 2003), 121.

Hildegard of Bingen. *Symphonia Armonie Celestium Revelationum,* translated by Barbara Newman (London and Ithaca, NY: Cornell UP, 1988), 129–31, 205.

______. "On the Three Qualities in a Flame," in *An Anthology of Christian Mysticism,* edited by Harvey Egan, SJ (Collegeville, MN: Liturgical Press, 1991), 203–4.

Howard, OSB, Katherine. *Praying with St. Benedict* (Winona, MN: Saint Mary's Press/Christian Brothers Publications, 1996), 82–83.

Huerre, OSB, Denis. *Letters to My Brothers and Sisters: Living by the Rule of St. Benedict,* translated by Sylvester Houédard, OSB (Collegeville, MN: Liturgical Press, 1994), 16.

Hume, OSB, Cardinal Basil. *The Intentional Life: The Making of a Spiritual Vocation* (Brewster, MA: Paraclete Press, 2003), 29.

______. *Searching for God* (New York/Ramsey, NJ: Paulist Press, 1977), 117–18.

Jebb, OSB, Philip. "Wonder Is so Sudden a Gift," in *A Touch of God: Eight Monastic Journeys,* edited by Maria Boulding (Still River, MA: St. Bede's, 1983), 23.

John of Fécamp. *Confessio Theologica,* quoted in *Spiritual Writers of the Middle Ages,* edited by Gerard Sitwell, OSB (New York: Hawthorn Books, 1961), 27–28.

Kownacki, OSB, Mary Lou. *Peace Is Our Calling: Contemporary Monasticism and the Peace Movement* (Erie, PA: Benet Press, 1981), 11.

LaTourrette, Victor-Antoine D'Avila. *A Monastic Year: Reflections from a Monastery* (Dallas, TX: Taylor, 1996), 152–53.

Leclercq, OSB, Jean. *The Love of Learning and the Desire for God: A Study of Monastic Culture*, translated by Catharine Misrahi (New York: Fordham University Press, 1960), 276–77.

Mabillon, OSB, Jean. *Treatise on Monastic Studies, 1696,* translated by John Paul McDonald (Lanham, MD, and Oxford, UK, 2004), 247.

Main, OSB, John. *Word into Silence* (New York/Ramsey, NJ: Paulist Press, 1981), 8.

Marmion, OSB, Columba, quoted in M. M. Philipon, OP, *The Spiritual Doctrine of Dom Marmion,* translated by Matthew Dillon, OSB (Westminster, MD: Newman Press, 1956), 158.

Mechthild of Magdeburg. *The Flowing Light of the Godhead,* in *The Fire and the Cloud: An Anthology of Catholic Spirituality,* edited by David A Fleming, SM (New York/Toronto/Ramsey, NJ: Paulist Press, 1978), 82.

———. "The Flowing Light of the Godhead," in *Mystics, Visionaries and Prophets: A Historical Anthology of Women's Spiritual Writings,* edited by Shawn Madigan, CSJ (Minneapolis: Fortress Press, 1988), 145.

Members of the Swiss-American Congregation. *Covenant of Peace: A Declaration on Monastic Life* (Conception, MO: Conception Abbey, 1975), 3.

Michel, OSB, Virgil, Basil Stegmann, OSB, and Sisters of St. Dominic. *Through Christ Our Lord* (New York: Macmillan, 1935), 50.

O'Keefe, OSB, Mark. *Priestly Wisdom: Insights from St. Benedict* (St. Meinrad, IN: Abbey Press, 2004), 86.

Peter Damian. "Letter," in *The Liturgy of The Hours,* vol. 3 (New York: Catholic Book Publishing, 1976), 1683.

Peter of Celle. *Monastic Discipline,* quoted in *Spiritual Writers of the Middle Ages,* edited by Gerard Sitwell, OSB (New York: Hawthorn Books, 1961), 37.

Rees, OSB, Daniel, and other members of the English Benedictine Congregation. *Consider Your Call: A*

Theology of Monastic Life Today (London: SPCK, 1978), 61.

The Rule of Benedict: A Guide to Christian Living. The Full Text of the Rule in Latin and English with Commentary by George Holzherr Abbot of Einsiedlen, translated by Monks of Glenstal Abbey (Dublin: Four Courts Press, 1994), 2.

Saint Benedict's Rule. translation and introduction by Patrick Barry, OSB, 2d edition. (New York/ Mahwah: HiddenSpring, 2004).

Skudlarek, OSB, William. *The Word in Worship: Preaching in a Liturgical Context* (Nashville: Abingdon, 1981), 80.

Stasiak, OSB, Kurt. The Things of God, a homily on Matthew 22:15–21, used with permission of the author.

Steindl-Rast, OSB, David. "Conclusions about a Beginning," in *Benedict's Dharma Buddists Reflect on the Rule of Saint Benedict,* edited by Patrick Henry (New York: Riverhead Books, 2001), 121–22.

Stewart, OSB, Columba. *Prayer and Community: The Benedictine Tradition* (Maryknoll, NY: Orbis Books, 1998), 75.

Theisen, OSB, Jerome. "Community as the Shape of Christian Salvation," in *The Continuing Quest for God: Monastic Spirituality in Tradition and Transition,* edited by William Skudlarenk, OSB (Collegeville, MN: Liturgical Press, 1982), 8.

Tinsely, OSB, Ambrose. *Pax: The Benedictine Way* (Collegeville, MN: Liturgical Press, 1994), 119.

Vogüé, Adalbert de. *To Love Fasting: The Monastic Experience,* translated by Jean Baptist Hasbrouck, OCSO (Petersham, MA: St. Bede Publications, 1994), 62.

Wright, OSB, Ralph. *Christ—Our Love for all Seasons: A Liturgy of the Hours for Everyone* (New York/Mahwah, NJ: Paulist Press, 2005), 151–52, 167–68, 63–64.

Acknowledgments

Hildegard of Bingen, "Antiphon for St. Boniface" and "Sequence for the Virgin," reprinted from Hildegard of Bingen, Barbara Newman, editor and translator: *Symphonia:* A critical edition of the *Symphonia armonie celestium revelationum.* Copyright © 1989 by Cornell University. Used by permission of the publisher, Cornell University Press.

"Blessed Trinity in One" from "On the Three Qualities of a Flame," by Hildegard of Bingen, from *An Anthology of Christian Mysticism,* ed. Harvey Egan, SJ, © copyright 1991 by Liturgical Press, pp. 203–204. Used with permission.

"Wonder Is So Sudden a Gift" by Philip Jebb, OSB, from *A Touch of God: Eight Monastic Journeys,* edited by Maria Boulding (Still River, MA: St Bede's, 1983), p. 23. Used by permission.

Creator alme siderum, anon., tr. Ralph Wright, OSB Copyright © 1989 by GIA Publications, Inc., 7404 S. Mason Ave., Chicago, IL 60638. www.giamusic.com 800.442.1358. All rights reserved. Used by permission.

Vexilla Regis, Venantius Honorius Fortunatus, tr. Ralph Wright, OSB Copyright © 1989 by GIA Publications, Inc., 7404 S. Mason Ave., Chicago, IL 60638. www.giamusic.com 800.442.1358. All rights reserved. Used by permission.

“We Watch for You, O Lord, Till Break of Day.” Text: Genevieve Glen, OSB, © 2002, Benedictine Nuns, Abbey of St. Walburga, Virginia Dale, CO. Published by OCP Publications, 5536 NE Hassalo, Portland OR 97213. Used with permission. All rights reserved.

“Let Us Boast Not in Foolishness.” Text: Genevieve Glen, OSB, © 2002, Benedictine Nuns, Abbey of St. Walburga, Virginia Dale, CO. Published by OCP Publications, 5536 NE Hassalo, Portland OR 97213. Used with permission. All rights reserved.

“Rejoice with All the Saints This Day.” Text ©) 2001, Harry Hagan, OSB. Published by OCP Publications, 5536 NE Hassalo, Portland OR 97213. All rights reserved. Used with permission.

Prayer “God of Truth and God of Beauty” from *Life Ablaze* by Joan Chittister, OSB, © 2001 by Sheed & Ward, an imprint of Rowman & Littlefield Publishing, Inc., p. 23. Used with permission.

“A Prayer to Make a Difference,” used with permission of Archbishop Daniel Buechlein, OSB.

Paulist Press is committed to preserving ancient forests and natural resources. We elected to print *Praying with the Benedictines* on 50% post consumer recycled paper, processed chlorine free. As a result, for this printing, we have saved:

5 Trees (40' tall and 6-8" diameter)
2,059 Gallons of Wastewater
828 Kilowatt Hours of Electricity
227 Pounds of Solid Waste
446 Pounds of Greenhouse Gases

Paulist Press made this paper choice because our printer, Thomson-Shore, Inc., is a member of Green Press Initiative, a nonprofit program dedicated to supporting authors, publishers, and suppliers in their efforts to reduce their use of fiber obtained from endangered forests.

For more information, visit www.greenpressinitiative.org